G-5280

THE BOOK OF
CHILDREN'S SONGTALES

Stories in Song

REVISED EDITION

Compiled by John M. Feierabend

GIA PUBLICATIONS, INC. · CHICAGO

Also by John M. Feierabend, published by GIA Publications, Inc.:
The Book of Fingerplays & Action Songs
The Book of Echo Songs
The Book of Call and Response
The Book of Beginning Circle Games
The Book of Songs and Rhymes with Beat Motions
The Book of Movement Exploration (*with Jane Kahan*)
The Book of Pitch Exploration

For infants and toddlers:
The Book of Lullabies
The Book of Wiggles & Tickles
The Book of Simple Songs & Circles
The Book of Bounces
The Book of Tapping & Clapping

On compact disc for infants and toddlers:
'Round and 'Round the Garden: Music in My First Year!
Ride Away on Your Horses: Music, Now I'm One!
Frog in the Meadow: Music, Now I'm Two!

On DVD and compact disc by Peggy Lyman and John M. Feierabend:
Move It! Expressive Movements with Classical Music
Move It 2! Expressive Movements with Classical Music

G-5280
The Book of Children's SongTales (Revised Edition)
Compiled by John M. Feierabend
www.giamusic.com/feierabend

Table of
Contents

Introduction

Stories help us make sense of our world and music speaks to our souls. The songs collected in this book are so engaging because they combine these two fundamental impulses.

This book contains wonderful stories in the form of songs. Just as children love to be read to, they also love being sung to, especially when the song tells a story. Passed down through the years, these Children's SongTales have withstood the test of time.

Generations of people from many different places have sung and enjoyed these songs. These SongTales have narratives that range from silly to sorrowful, from straightforward to satirical. All are delicious! Each song will generate wonderful images in a child's imagination.

A loving adult who reads to a child with feeling helps that child to understand the expressiveness possible on the printed page. That child will then be more likely to bring the same intuitive understanding to his or her own reading, and will grow up to bring more depth, emotion, and nuance to the words he or she reads.

These SongTales provide a child's first experience of narrative and artful expressiveness in music. Children who hear these songs sung with expression will later be expressive singers themselves and will appreciate the expressiveness in other musical performances.

So, come and enjoy these songs. Sing them with spirit. You and your children will want to hear them again and again!

John M. Feierabend

Love and Marriage

The Old Woman's Courtship

Boys:
"Old wom-an, old wom-an, will you go a-shear-ing?

Old wom-an, old wom-an, will you go a-shear-ing?"

Girls:
Speak a lit-tle loud-er, sir, I'm rath-er hard of hear-ing.

Speak a lit-tle loud-er, sir, I'm rath-er hard of hear-ing.

Additional Verses

2. "Old woman, old woman, are you good at spinning?"...
"Speak a little louder, sir, I'm rather hard of hearing."...

3. "Old woman, old woman, can you do fine weaving?"...
"Speak a little louder, sir, I'm rather hard of hearing."...

4. "Old woman, old woman, will you darn my stockings?"...
"Speak a little louder, sir, I think I almost hear you."...

5. "Old woman, old woman, why don't we get married?"...
"Lordy, mercy on my soul, I'm sure that now I hear you!"...

Froggie Went A-courtin'

Frog - gie went a - court - in' and   he did ride a -

huf,   a - huh.   Frog - gie went a - court - in' and

he did ride, Sword and pis - tol by his side, a - huh.____

* *

Additional Verses

2. He rode up to Miss Mouse's door,
   a huh.
   He rode up to Miss Mouse's door,
   Where he'd been many times
   before, a huh.

3. He said, "Miss Mouse, are you
   within?"....
   "Yes, kind sir, I sit and spin."....

4. He took Miss Mouse upon his
   knee....
   Said, "Miss Mouse, will you marry
   me?"....

5. "Without my Uncle Rat's
   consent....
   I would not marry the President"....

6. Uncle Rat laughed and shook his
   fat sides....
   To think his niece would be a
   bride....

7. Then Uncle Rat rode off to
   town....
   To buy his niece a wedding gown....

8. "Where will the wedding breakfast
   be?"....
   "Way down yonder in the hollow
   tree"....

9. "What will the wedding breakfast
   be?"....
   "Fried mosquito and a black-eyed
   pea"....

10. The first to come was the little
    white moth....
    She spread out the tablecloth....

11. The next to come was the
    bumblebee....
    Played the fiddle upon his knee....

12. The next to come was a little
    flea....
    Danced a jig with the bumble
    bee....

13. The next to come was Mrs.
    Cow....
    Tried to dance but didn't know
    how....

14. Now Mister Froggie was dressed
    in green....
    Sweet Miss Mousie looked like a
    queen....

15. In slowly walked the Parson
    Rook....
    Under his arm he carried a
    book....

16. They gathered 'round the lucky
    pair....
    Singing, dancing, everywhere....

17. Then Froggie and Mouse went
    off to France....
    That's the end of my romance....

Alternative Ending

17. They all went sailing across the
    lake....
    And got swallowed by a big black
    snake....

18. There's bread and cheese upon
    the shelf....
    If you want any more you can
    sing it yourself....

* *

Fiddle-Dee-Dee

Fid - dle - dee - dee, fid - dle - dee - dee, the
fly has mar - ried the bum - ble - bee. Said the
fly, said he, "Will you mar - ry me. And live with me sweet
bum - ble-bee?" Fid - dle - dee - dee, Fid - dle - dee - dee, the
fly has mar - ried the bum - ble - bee.

Additional Verses

2. Fiddle-dee-dee, fiddle-dee-dee,
   The fly has married the bumblebee.
   Said the bee, said she, "I'll live
      under your wing,
   And you'll never know I carry a sting."
   Fiddle-dee-dee, fiddle-dee-dee,
   The fly has married the bumblebee.

3. Fiddle-dee-dee...
   So when the Parson Beetle had
      joined the pair,
   They both went out to take the air.
      Fiddle-dee-dee...

4. Fiddle-dee-dee...
   And the flies did buzz and the bells
      did ring,
   Did you ever hear so merry a thing?
      Fiddle-dee-dee...

5. Fiddle-dee-dee...
   And then to think that of all that
      flies,
   The bumblebee should carry the
      prize.
   Fiddle-dee-dee...

'Twas on a Monday Morning

'Twas on a (Mon-day) morn - ing, When I be-held my

dar - ling, She looked so neat and charm - ing, In

ev - 'ry high de - gree.___ She looked so neat and

nim - ble, Oh, (a - wash - ing of) her lin - en, Oh.

Dash-ing a - way with the smooth-ing iron, Dash-ing a - way with the

smooth - ing iron, She stole my heart a - way.___

2. ...Tuesday...*a-starching of...*
3. ...Wednesday...*a-hanging out...*
4. ...Thursday...*a-ironing of...*
5. ...Friday...*a-folding of...*
6. ...Saturday...*a-airing of...*
7. ...Sunday...*a-wearing of...*

Pantomime the motions of each action
with the beat of the song.

The Frog and the Mouse

There was a frog lived in a well,

Whip - see did - dle dee dan - dy O! There

was a mouse lived in a mill, Whip - see did - dle dee

dan - dy O! This frog he would a - woo - ing ride, With

sword and pis - tol by his side, With a har - um scar - um

did - dle dum dar - um, Whip - see did - dle dee dan - dy O!

Verse 2

He rode 'til he came to Mouse's
 Hall,
Whipsee diddle dee dandy O!
Where he most tenderly did call.
Whipsee diddle dee dandy O!
"O Mistress Mouse, are you at
 home?
And if you are, oh, please come
 down."
With a harum scarum diddle dum
 darum,
Whipsee diddle dee dandy O.

Verse 3

"My Uncle Rat is not at home,"....
"I dare not for my life come down."....
Then Uncle Rat he soon comes home,
"And who's been here since I've been gone?"....

Verse 4

"Here's been a fine young gentleman,...."
"Who swears he'll have me if he can."....
Then Uncle Rat gave his consent
And made a handsome settlement....

Verse 5

Four partridge pies with season made,....
Two potted larks and marmalade,....
Four woodcocks and a venison pie.
I would that at that feast were I....

Lazy John

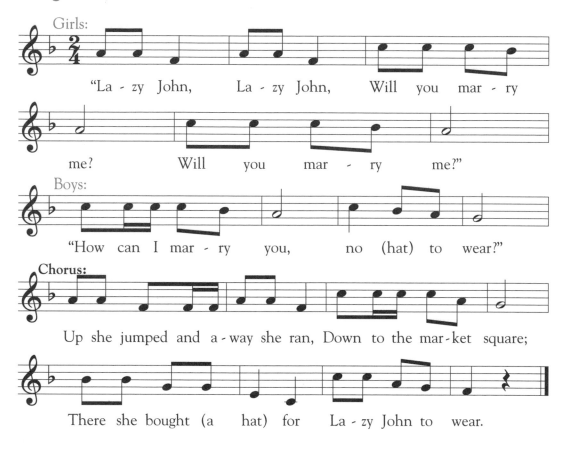

Girls:
"La - zy John, La - zy John, Will you mar - ry me? Will you mar - ry me?"

Boys:
"How can I mar - ry you, no (hat) to wear?"

Chorus:
Up she jumped and a - way she ran, Down to the mar - ket square; There she bought (a hat) for La - zy John to wear.

(For each verse, change the following word)

2. ...shirt *...a shirt....*
3. ...pants *...some pants....*
4. ...socks *...some socks....*
5. ...shoes *...some shoes....*
6. *(See below)*

Boys (last time):
"How can I mar - ry you, With a wife and ten chil - dren at home?"

Soldier, Soldier

"O sol-dier, sol-dier won't you mar-ry me, with your

musk-et, fife, and drum?" "Oh, no sweet maid, I

can-not mar-ry you for I have no (shirt) to put on." So

up she went to her grand-fa-ther's chest and she

found him (a shirt) of the ver-y, ver-y best, Yes, she

found him (a shirt) of the ver-y, ver-y best and the

sol-dier put them— on.

2. ...pants   ...some pants....
3. ...shoes   ...some shoes....
4. ...coat   ...a coat....
5. ...hat   ...a hat....
6. ...gloves   ...some gloves....

7. "Now, soldier, soldier won't you marry me with your musket, fife, and drum?"

"Oh, no sweet maid, I cannot marry you, for I have a wife of my own."

Risseldy Rosseldy

I mar-ried my wife in the month of June,

Ris-sel-dy, Ros-sel-dy, mow, mow, mow. I car-ried her off in a

sil-ver spoon, Ris-sel-dy, Ros-sel-dy, mow, mow, mow.

Refrain

Ris-sel-dy Ros-sel-dy, hey bom-bas-si-ty, nick-e-ty, nack-e-ty,

Ret-ri-cal qual-i-ty, Wil-low-by, Wal-low-by mow, mow, mow.

Additional Verses

2. She combed her hair but once a year,
Risseldy, Rosseldy, mow, mow, mow.
With every rake she shed a tear,
Risseldy, Rosseldy, mow, mow, mow.
(Refrain)

3. She churned the butter in Dad's
old boot....
And for a dasher, used her foot.....
(Refrain)

4. The butter came out grizzly gray....
The cheese took legs and ran
away....
(Refrain)

5. She swept the floor but once a
year....
And for a broom she used a chair....
(Refrain)

6. She kept her shoes on the pantry
shelf....
If you want any more you can
sing it yourself....

Robin a Thrush

Rob - in a Thrush, he mar - ried a wife, With a

pop - pe - ty, pop - pe - ty now, now. She proved to be the

plague of his life, With a hie, jig jig - ge - ty,

ruf - fe - ty pet - ti - coat, Rob - in a Thrush cries now, now.

Additional Verses

2. She never got up till twelve o'clock,
with a poppety, poppety, now, now,
now.
And when she got up, she wound
up the clock,
With a hie, jig jiggety, ruffety petticoat,
Robin a thrush cries now, now.

3. She swept the house but once a
year....
The reason was that brooms were
dear....

4. She milked her cows but once a
week....
The reason was she liked milk sweet....

5. The butter she made in the old
man's boot....
And for want of a churn, she clapt
in her foot....

6. Her cheese, when made, was put
on the shelf....
It never was turned till it turned
itself....

7. It turned and it turned till it rolled
on the floor....
It stood upon legs and it walked to
the door....

8. It walked till it came to Banbury
Fair....
And the dame followed after upon
a gray mare....

The Leather-Winged Bat

"Hi," said the lit-tle brown leath-er winged bat,

"I'll tell you the rea-son that, The rea-son that I

fly in the night's, be-cause I lost my heart's de-light."

Chorus:

How-dee-dow dee did-dle-o-day, How-dee-dow dee did-dle-o-day,

How-dee-dow-dee did-dle-o-day, How dow dee-dih die-do do.

Additonal Verses

2. "Hi," said the woodpecker, sittin'
on a fence,
"Once I courted a handsome finch.
She got sulky and from me fled,
Ever since then my head's been red."
(*Chorus*)

3. "Hi," said the little mourning dove,
"I'll tell you how to regain your love.
Court her by night and court her by
day.
Never give her time to say, "O Nay!"
(*Chorus*)

4. "Hi," said the bluejay as she flew,
"If I were young, then I'd have two.
If one got saucy and wanted to go,
I'd have a new string for my bow."
(*Chorus*)

5. "Hi," said the owl with eyes so big,
"If I had a hen, I'd feed her like a
pig,
But here I sit on a frozen lake,
Which causes my poor heart to
break."
(*Chorus*)

6. *Repeat first verse.*

The Crabfish

There was a lit-tle man and he had a lit-tle wife and he

loved her as much as he loved his life. **Refrain:** Mash a

row dow dow dow did-dle all the day, Mash a

row dow dow dow did-dle all the day.

Additinal Verses

2. One hour in the night, his wife
   grew sick,
   And all that she wanted was a little
   crab fish...

3. Then her husband arose and put
   on his clothes,
   And down to the seaside he
   followed his nose...

4. "O fisherman. O fisherman, can
   you tell me,
   Have you a little crabfish you could
   sell to me?"...

5. "O yes, O yes. I have one, two, and
   three,
   And the best of them I will sell to
   thee"...

6. So he caught him and bought him
   and put him in a dish,
   And he said, "Oh wife, put your
   nose to this."...

7. The his wife just to smell him
   popped up from her clothes,
   And the crabfish popped up and
   grabbed her by the nose...

8. "Oh help, dear husband; come
   hither, do you hear?"
   But the crabfish had already
   grabbed him by the ear...

9. And so my friends, if for a crabfish
   you thirst;
   Please try to remember to cook him
   first...

Who's Who?

Songs about people

King Arthur

When good King Ar - thur ruled this land, He

was a good - ly king, He

stole three pecks of bar - ley - meal, To

make a bag pud - ding.

Verse 2

A bag pudding the Queen did make,
And stuffed it well with plums,
And in it put great lumps of fat,
As big as my two thumbs.

Verse 3

The King and Queen did eat thereof,
And noblemen beside,
And what they could not eat that
  night,
The Queen next morning fried.

There Was an Old Woman

There was an old wom-an all skin and bones.

Oo - oo - oo - oo.

Additional Verses

2. One day she thought she'd take a walk...
3. She went down by the old graveyard...
4. She saw some bones a-laying around...
5. She went to the closet to get a broom...
6. She opened the door and - "BOO!"

Maschero   *French Sailing Song*

Al - lee,   Al - loe   for   Mas - cher - o;*

Al - lee,   al - lee,   al - loe.   He

eats   the   meat   and   gives   us   the   bones.

Al - lee,   al - lee,   al - lee   al - loe.

Al - lee,   al - lee   al - loe.

Verse 2

Allee, alloe for Maschero,
Allee, allee, alloe,
We ask for bread, he gives us a stone.
Allee, allee, allee, alloe,
Allee, allee, alloe.

Verse 3

....If he would ride then we must
    row....

Verse 4

....If we say "yes" then he says "no"....

Verse 5

....If we would stay then he would
    go....

"Maschero" is the captain of the ship.

There Was Once a Princess

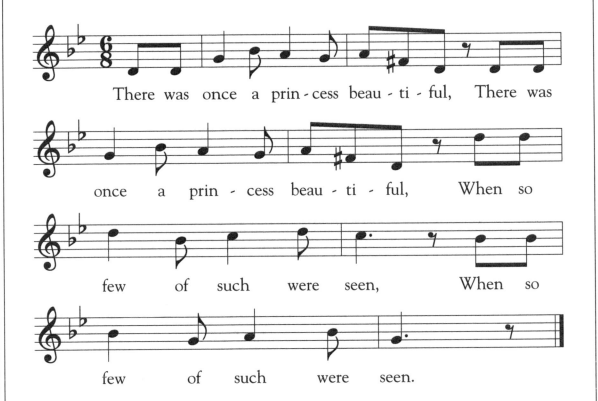

There was once a prin - cess beau - ti - ful, There was

once a prin - cess beau - ti - ful, When so

few of such were seen, When so

few of such were seen.

Additional Verses

2. A spell was cast upon her,
   A spell was cast upon her,
   When so few of such were seen,
   When so few of such were seen.

3. The castle was enchanted....

4. A hundred years she slept there....

5. The thorns grew thick around her....

6. A handsome prince came riding....

7. He chopped the thorns down, one by one....

8. He woke the sleeping princess....

9. They had a royal wedding....

Jennie Jenkins

"Will you wear white, Oh my dear, Oh my dear? Oh, will you wear white— Jen - nie Jen - kins?" "I won't wear white for the col - or's too bright," I'll— buy me a fol - de - rol - dy til - de - tol - dy, seek a dou - ble roll,_____ Jen - nie Jen - kins, roll.

Additional Verses

2. "Will you wear red, Oh my dear,
   Oh my dear?
   Will you wear red Jennie Jenkins?"
   "I won't wear red, it's the color of
   my head."
   I'll buy me a folderoldy, tildetoldy,
   Seek a double roll, Jennie Jenkins, roll.

3. "Will you wear blue"...."I will wear
   blue, if your love is true"....

4. "Will you wear green"...."I won't wear
   green, it's a shame to be seen"....

5. "Will you wear purple"...."I won't
   wear purple, it's the color of a
   turtle"....

6. "Will you wear black"...."I won't
   wear black, it's the color of my
   back"....

7. "What will you wear"...."I have
   nothing to wear, I can't go any
   where"....

Clever Beasties

Songs about animals

The Farmyard

Up went I to my fa-ther's farm, on a May day morn-ing ear - ly. Feed - ing all my fa - ther's (cows) on a May day morn - ing ear - ly. With a (moo moo) here, and a (moo moo) there, here a (moo), there a (moo), here a pret-ty (moo). Six jol-ly maids come dance a - long with me, To the mer - ry green fields of the farm - yard.

Create additional verses with other animals and
their sounds, such as horses, cats, dogs, sheep, etc.

Don Gato *Mexican*

Es - ta - ba el ga - to sen - ta - do_____ en

su si - lli - ta de pa - lo_____ con

som - bre - ri - to de pa - ja_____ co - mo

va - lien - te sol - da - do._____

Verse 2

Llególe carta de España
Que si quería ser casado
Con la gatita morisca
Del ojito aceitunado.

Verse 3

Su papa dijo que sí.
Su mama dijo que no.
Y el gatito de cuidado
Del tejado se cayó.

Verse 4

Médicos y cirujanos,
Vengan a curar al gato,
Procuren que se confiese
De lo que se haya robado:

Repeat last two musical phrases:
Salchichón de la despensa
Y la carne del tejado.

From *El Patio de Mi Casa* (G-6947). Used with permission.

Translation

Verse 1
The cat was sitting down
In his little chair made of sticks
With his little straw hat
Like a valiant soldier.

Verse 2
A letter arrived from Spain
Asking him if he wanted to marry
The Moorish cat
With olive-colored eyes.

Verse 3
His father said yes.
His mother said no.
And the cat, not being careful,
Fell from the roof.

Verse 4
The doctors and surgeons
Went to cure the cat,
To get a confession
For what he had stolen:

A sausage from the pantry
And the meat from the roof.

The Fox

There was an old fox and he had a lov-ing wife, And he went out one moon shin-y night Think-ing to get some-thing ve-ry, ve-ry nice, Be-fore he lay down in his den, O!

Verse 2

He went on till he came to a yard,
Where there were fat ducks and geese
   to be had,
He swore the fattest should grease his
   beard,
Before he lay down in his den, O!

Verse 3

He took the gray goose by the neck,
And he threw her across his back,
And as he went along she went,
   "Quack, quack,"
And her legs hung dangling down, O!

Verse 4

He went on till he came to his den,
When he had little ones, eight, nine,
   and ten,
"Oh, father Reynard, where have
   you been?
You have been to some lucky yard, O!"

Verse 5

(The following is sung to the tune of the last two lines)

Then they took the gray goose, and
   they dragged her in,
And so merrily they picked her
   bones, O!

Kitty Alone

Saw a crow a fly-ing low, kit-ty a-lone, kit-ty a-lone;

Saw a crow a fly-ing low, kit-ty a-lone, a-lye;

Saw a crow a fly-ing low, And a cat a-spin-ning tow,

Kit-ty a-lone, a-lye; Rock-um-a-rye-ree.

Verse 2

In came a little bat, kitty alone, kitty alone;
In came a little bat, kitty alone, a-lye;
In came a little bat with some butter and some fat,
Kitty alone, a-lye; Rock-um-a-rye-ree.

Verse 3

Next came in was a honeybee....
with a fiddle across his knee....

Verse 4

Next came in was little Pete....
fixing around to go to sleep....
(make up additional verses then end with:)

Verse 5

Bee-o, bye-o, baby-o, kitty alone, kitty alone;
Bee-o, bye-o, baby-o, kitty alone, a-lye;
Bee-o, bye-o, baby-o, bee-o, bye-o, baby-o,
Kitty alone, a-lye; rock-um-a-rye-ree.

The Fox Went Out

The fox went out— on a chil-ly night, He prayed for the moon to give him light, For he'd man-y a mile to go that night be-fore he reached the town - o, town - o, town - o, he'd man-y a mile— to go that night be-fore he reached the town - o.

Additional Verses

2. He ran till he came to a great big bin,
   The ducks and the geese were put
       therein,
   Said, "A couple of you will grease my
       chin
   Before I reach the town-o, town-o,
       town-o,
   A couple of you will grease my chin
       before I leave this town-o."

3. He grabbed the gray goose by the neck,
   Slung the little one over his back,
   He didn't mind their "Quack-quack-
       quack,"
   And the legs all dangling down-o...

4. Then old Mother Pitter-Patter
       jumped out of bed;
   Out of the window she cocked her
       head,
   Crying, "John, John, the gray goose is
       gone
   And the fox is on the town-o,"...

5. Then John, he went to the top of
       the hill,
   Blew his horn both loud and shrill;
   The fox, he said, "I better flee with
       my kill,
   He'll soon be on my trail-o,"...

6. He ran till he came to his cozy
       den.
   There were the little ones, eight,
       nine, ten.
   They said, "Daddy, you better go
       back again,
   'Cause it looks like a mighty fine
       town-o,"...

7. Then the fox and his wife without
       any strife,
   Cut up the goose with fork and
       knife,
   They never had such a supper in
       their life,
   And the little ones chewed on the
       bones-o, ...

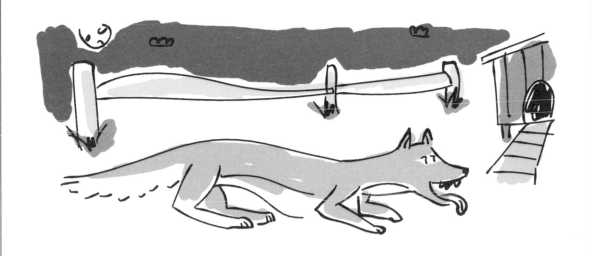

Long Time Ago

Once there was a lit-tle kit-ty,—— White as the snow. She went out to hunt a mou-sie,—— Long time a-go.

Verse 2

Two black eyes had little kitty,
Black as a crow,
And she spied a little mousie,
Long time ago.

Verse 3

Four soft paws had little kitty,
Soft as the snow,
And they caught the little mousie,
Long time ago.

Verse 4

Nine pearl teeth had little kitty,
All in a row,
And they bit the little mousie,
Long time ago.

Verse 5

When the kitty bit the mousie,
Mousie cried out, "Oh!"
But she got away from kitty,
Long time ago.

The North Wind Doth Blow

The north wind doth blow, And we shall have snow, And

what will the rob - in do then, poor thing? He'll

sit in a barn, to keep him - self warm, And

hide his head un - der his wing, poor thing.

Verse 2

The north wind doth blow
And we shall have snow,
And what will the swallow do then,
    poor thing?
Oh, do you not know,
He's gone long ago
To a country where he will find
    spring, poor thing.

Verse 3

The north wind doth blow,
And we shall have snow,
And what will the doormouse do
    then, poor thing?
He'll curl up in a ball
In his nest snug and small;
He'll sleep till warm weather comes
    in, poor thing.

Little Black Bull

The lit-tle black bull came down the mead-ow,

Hoo - sen John - ny, Hoo - sen John - ny. The

lit - tle black bull came down the mead - ow,

Long time a - go. Long time a - go,

Long time a - go. The lit - tle black bull came

down the mead - ow long time a - go.

Verse 2

First he pawed and then he bellowed,
Hoosen Johnny, Hoosen Johnny.
First he pawed and then he bellowed,
  long time ago.
Long time ago, long time ago.
First he pawed and then he bellowed,
  long time ago.

Verse 3

He shook his tail and jarred the river,
Hoosen Johnny, Hoosen Johnny
He shook his tail and jarred the river,
  long time ago.
Long time ago, long time ago.
He shook his tail and jarred the river,
  long time ago.

Verse 4

He whet his horn on a white-oak
  sapling...

Verse 5

He pawed the dirt in the heifers'
  faces...

There Was a Bullfrog

There was a bull - frog liv - ing in the spring,

Sing song Pol - ly won't you ky - me - o. He

had such a cold that he could not sing, Sing song Pol-ly won't you

Chorus

ky - me - o. Kee - mo, ky - mo, dar - o - wah, Ma-

hee, ma - hi, ma - ho, Nit cap ko bom - a - did - dle,

Nit cap set back, Sing song Pol - ly won't you ky - me - o.

Verse 2

Oh, I took him out and laid him on
   the ground,
Sing Sing Polly won't you kymeo.
The bullfrog winked and looked all
   around,
Sing Sing Polly won't you kymeo.
   (*Chorus*)

Verse 3

He rode away to get him a bride....
With a sword and a pistol by his side....
   (*Chorus*)

Verse 4

But the sun shone bright for there was
   no rain....
So the bullfrog jumped in the pond
   again....
   (*Chorus*)

Three Little Kittens

Three lit - tle kit - tens, they lost their mit - tens and

they be - gan to cry. "Oh, Moth - er dear, we sad - ly fear our

mit - tens we have lost." — "What! lost your mit - tens, you

naugh - ty kit - tens! Then you shall have no pie. —

Me - ow, me - ow. Then you shall have no pie." —

Verse 2

Three little kittens, they found their
  mittens, and they began to cry.
"Oh, Mother dear, see here, see here,
  our mittens we have found."
"Put on your mittens, you silly kittens
  and you shall have some pie."
"Purr, purr, oh, let us have some pie."

Verse 3

Three little kittens put on their
  mittens, and soon ate up the pie.
"Oh, Mother dear, we greatly fear our
  mittens we have soiled."
"What! soiled your mittens, you

naughty kittens!" Then they began to
  sigh.
"Meow, meow." Then they began to
  sigh.

Verse 4

Three little kittens, they washed their
  mittens, and hung them out to dry.
"Oh, Mother dear, do you not hear,
  our mittens we have washed?"
"What! washed your mittens, then
  you're good kittens, but I smell a
  rat close by."
"Meow, meow. We smell a rat
  close by."

The Derby Ram

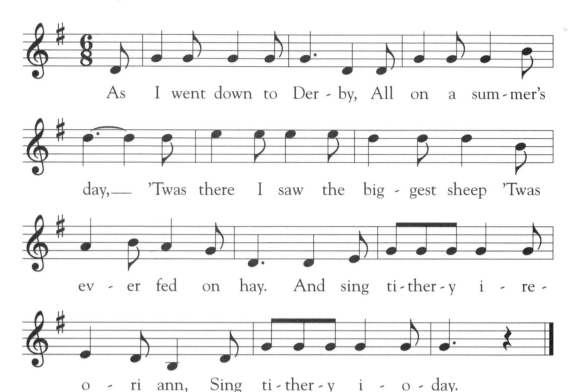

As I went down to Der-by, All on a sum-mer's day,— 'Twas there I saw the big-gest sheep 'Twas ev-er fed on hay. And sing ti-ther-y i re-o-ri ann, Sing ti-ther-y i o-day.

Verse 2

The wool on that sheep's back, sir,
It reached unto the sky,
The eagles built their nests there,
I heard the young ones cry.
And sing tithery ireori ann,
Sing tithery ioday.

Verse 3

The horn on the that sheep's head, sir,
It reached up to the moon,
A man went up in February,
And never came down till June.
And sing....

Verse 4

The wool on that ram's belly,
It dragged down to the ground,

They sold it there in Derby,
For forty thousand pounds.
And sing....

Verse 5

He had four feet to walk, sir,
He had four feet to stand,
And every foot he had, sir,
Took at least an acre of land.
And sing....

Verse 6

The wool on that ram's tail, sir,
I've heard the weaver say,
It spun full forty yards, sir,
And some was thrown away.
And sing....

A-One, A-Two, A-Three

Counting songs

Over in the Meadow

O-ver in the mead-ow, in the sand in the sun, Lived an

old moth-er tur-tle and her lit-tle tur-tle one.

"Dig," said the moth-er, "I dig," said the one. So he

dug and was glad in the sand in the sun.

Additional Verses

2. Over in the meadow where the tall
   grasses grew,
   Lived an old mother fox and her
   little foxes two.
   "Run," said the mother. "We run,"
   said the two;
   So they ran and were glad where
   the tall grasses grew.

3. Over in the meadow in a nest in
   the tree,
   Lived an old mother robin and her
   little birdies three.

"Sing," said the mother. "We sing,"
said the three;
So they sang and were glad in that
nest in the tree.

4. Over in the meadow in a tall
   sycamore,
   Lived an old mother chipmunk and
   her little chipmunks four.
   "Play," said the mother. "We play,"
   said the four;
   So they played and were glad in
   that tall sycamore.

5. Over in the meadow in a new little
   hive,
   Lived an old mother bee and her
   honeybees five.
   "Bzzz," said the mother. "We bzzz,"
   said the five;
   So they bzzzed and were glad in
   their new little hive.

6. Over in the meadow in a dam built
   of sticks,
   Lived an old mother beaver and
   her little beavers six.
   "Build," said the mother. "We
   build," said the six;
   So they built and were glad in the
   dam built of sticks.

7. Over in the meadow in the green
   wet bogs,
   Lived an old mother froggie and
   her seven polliwogs.
   "Swim," said the mother. "We
   swim," said the 'wogs;
   So they swam and were glad in the
   green wet bogs.

8. Over in the meadow as the day
   grew late,
   Lived an old mother owl and her
   little owls eight.
   "Wink," said the mother. "We
   wink," said the eight;
   So they winked and were glad as
   the day grew late.

9. Over in the meadow in a web on
   the pine,
   Lived an old mother spider and her
   little spiders nine.
   "Spin," said the mother. "We spin,"
   said the nine;
   So they spun and were glad in their
   web on the pine.

10. Over in the meadow in a warm
    little den,
    Lived an old mother rabbit and her
    little bunnies ten.
    "Hop," said the mother. "We hop,"
    said the ten;
    So they hopped and were glad in
    their warm little den.

The Keeper

The keep - er would a - hunt - ing go, And under his coat he car - ried a bow, All for to shoot at a mer - ry lit - tle doe, A - mong the leaves so— green, O!

Refrain

Jack - ie boy! *Mas - ter!* Sing ye well? *Ver - y well.* Hey down! *Ho down!* Der - ry der - ry down. A - mong the leaves so— green, O. To my hey down, down! *To my ho down, down!* Hey down! *Ho down!* Der - ry der - ry down, A - mong the leaves so— green, O!

Italicized words are sung by a solo voice.

Verse 2

The first doe he shot at he missed.
The second one he trimmed and
 kissed.
The third one went where nobody
 wist,
Among the leaves so green, O!
 (*Refrain*)

Verse 3

The fourth doe, she did cross the
 plain,
The keeper fetched her back again,
Where she is now, she may remain,
Among the leaves so green, O!
 (*Refrain*)

Verse 4

The fifth doe, she did cross the brook,
The keeper fetched her back with his
 crook.
Where she is now, you must go look,
Among the leaves so green, O!
 (*Refrain*)

Verse 5

The sixth doe she ran over the plain,
But he with his hounds did turn her
 again,
And it's there he did hunt in a merry,
 merry vein,
Among the leaves green, O!
 (*Refrain*)

One Wide River

Old No-ah built him-self an ark, *one more riv-er to cross,*

He built it out of hick-o-ry bark, *one more riv-er to cross.*

One wide riv-er,— and that wide riv-er is Jor-dan.

One wide riv-er,— there's one more riv-er to cross.—

Additonal Verses

2. The animals came in two by two,
   one more river to cross,
   The elephant and the kangaroo,
   one more river to cross…
   (Refrain)

3. The animals came in three by three...
   The big baboon and the
   chimpanzee...
   (Refrain)

4. The animals came in four by four...
   Old Noah got mad and hollered for
   more...
   (Refrain)

5. The animals came in five by five...
   The bees came swarming from the
   hive...
   (Refrain)

6. The animals came in six by six...
   The lion laughed at the monkey's
   tricks...
   (Refrain)

7. When Noah found he had no sail...
   He just ran up his old coat tail...
   (Refrain)

8. Before the voyage did begin...
   Old Noah pulled the gangplank
   in...
   (Refrain)

9. They never knew where they
   were at...
   Till the old ark bumped on
   Ararat...
   (Refrain)

A Riddle and Three Swaps

The Riddle Song

I gave my love a cher-ry that has no stone, I gave my love a chick-en that has no— bone, I gave my love a ring— that has no end, I gave my love a ba-by with no cry-in'.

Verse 2

How can there be a cherry that has
no stone?
How can there be a chicken that has
no bone?
How can there be a ring that has no
end?
How can there be a baby with no
cryin'?

Verse 3

A cherry, when it's blooming, it has
no stone,
A chicken when it's pipping, it has
no bone,
A ring when it's rolling, it has no
end,
A baby when it's sleeping, has no
cryin'.

The Swapping Song

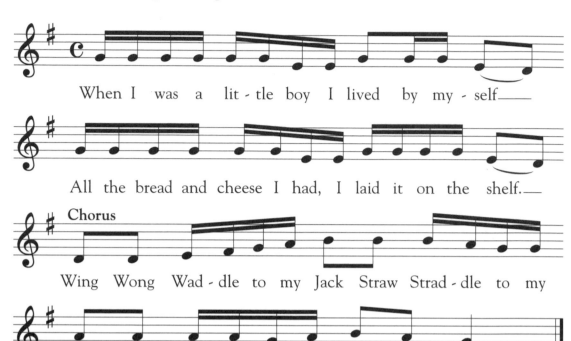

When I was a lit-tle boy I lived by my-self

All the bread and cheese I had, I laid it on the shelf.

Chorus

Wing Wong Wad-dle to my Jack Straw Strad-dle to my

John Fair Fad-dle to my long ways home.

Additional Verses

2. The rats and the mice they led me
   such a life,
   I had to go to London to get me a
   wife.
   (Chorus)

3. The roads were so muddy and the
   lanes were so narrow,
   Had to bring her home in an old
   wheelbarrow.
   (Chorus)

4. Wheelbarrow broke and my wife
   got a fall,
   Down came the wheelbarrow, little
   wife and all.
   (Chorus)

5. Swapped my wheelbarrow, got me
   a horse,
   Then I rode from course to course.
   (Chorus)

6. Swapped my horse and got me a
   mare,
   Then I rode from fair to fair.
   (Chorus)

7. Swapped my mare and got me a
   cow,
   In that trade I learned just how.
   (Chorus)

8. Swapped my cow and got me a
   calf,
     In that trade I just lost half.
     (*Chorus*)

9. Swapped my calf and got me a
   sheep,
     Then I rode myself to sleep.
     (*Chorus*)

10. Swapped my sheep and got me a
    hen,
      O what a pretty thing I had then.
      (*Chorus*)

11. Swapped my hen and got me a
    rat,
      Put it on the haystack away from
      the cat.
      (*Chorus*)

12. Swapped my rat and got me a
    mouse,
      Tail caught afire and burned up
      my house.
      (*Chorus*)

13. Swapped my mouse and got me a
    mole,
      The doggoned thing went straight
      to its hole.
      (*Chorus*)

The Sow Took the Measles

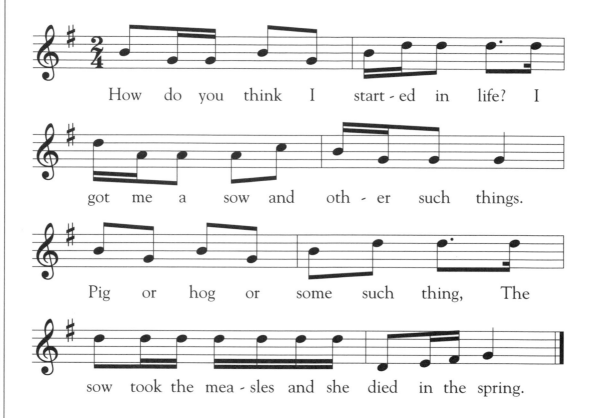

How do you think I start-ed in life? I got me a sow and oth-er such things. Pig or hog or some such thing, The sow took the mea-sles and she died in the spring.

Verse 2

What do you think I did with her hide?
Made the best saddle you ever did ride.
Saddle or bridle or some such thing,
The sow took the measles and she died in the spring.

Verse 3

What do you think I did with her tail?
Made me a whip and also a flail.
Whip or whip-handle, some such thing....

Verse 4

What do you think I made with her hair?
Made the best *stain you ever did wear.
Satin or silk or some such thing....

Verse 5

What do you think I did with her feet?
Made the best pickle you ever did eat.
Pickle or glue or some such thing....

*dye

And So On And So On

Old MacDonald

Old Mac-Don-ald had a farm, E-I-E-I-O. And

on his farm he had some (ducks), E-I-E-I-O. With a

("Quack, quack"), here and a ("Quack, quack"), there.

Here a ("Quack"), there a ("Quack"), ev'-ry-where a ("Quack, quack").

Old Mac-Don-ald had a farm, E-I-E-I-O.

Add additional animals for each verse.
Repeat these lines as each animal is added.

Had a Little Rooster

1. Had a lit-tle roost-er and my roost-er pleased me.

Fed my roost-er 'neath yon - der tree,

That lit-tle roost-er went, "Cock - a - doo-dle doo, Dee -

doo - dle, dee - doo - dle, dee - doo - dle, dee - do."

2. Had a lit-tle cat and my cat pleased me.

Fed my cat___ 'neath yon - der tree.

That lit-tle cat___ went, "Meow, meow, meow."

That lit-tle roost-er went, "Cock - a - doo-dle doo, Dee

doo - dle, dee - doo - dle, dee - doo - dle, dee - do."

Additional Verses

3. Had a little dog and my dog
   pleased me,
   Fed my dog 'neath yonder tree,
   That little dog went, "Arf, arf, arf,"
   That little cat went, "Meow, meow,
   meow,"
   That little rooster went, "Cock-a-
   doodle-doo, Dee doodle-dee,
   doodle-dee, doodle-dee doo."

4. ...duck went, "Quack, quack, quack"....

5. ...pig went, "Oink, oink, oink"....

6. ...sheep went, "Baa, baa, baa"....

7. ...cow went, "Moo, moo, moo"....

8. ...horse went, "Neigh, neigh, neigh"....

Bought Me a Cat

1. Bought me a cat, my cat pleased me,
Fed my cat un - der yon - der tree.
Cat went, "Fid - dle - i - fee."

2. Bought me a (hen), my (hen) pleased me.
Fed my (hen) un - der yon - der tree.
(Hen) went, ("Chip - sy, chip - sy"),
cat went, "Fid - dle - i - fee."

Additional Verses

3. duck...."Slishy, sloshy"....
4. goose...."Qua, qua"....
5. dog...."Bow, wow"....
6. sheep...."Baa, baa"....

7. cow...."Moo, moo"....
8. horse...."Neigh, neigh"....
9. baby...."Mommy, mommy"....
10. wife...."Honey, honey"....

Oh, In the Woods

Oh,   in the woods there was   a   tree. The nic-est tree that

e're   you   saw. And the   tree   was   in   the   wood   and   the

wood   lies   down   in   the   val-ley - o.——   And the

wood   lies   down   in   the   val-ley - o.——

* The melody between the asterisks is repeated as many times as is necessary.

Additional Verses

2. And on that tree there was a
   branch,
   The nicest branch that e're you saw,
   And the branch was on the tree,
   And the tree was in the wood,
   And the wood lies down in the
   valley-o,
   And the wood lies down in the
   valley-o.

3. And on that branch there was a
   nest...

4. And in that nest there was an
   egg...

5. And in that egg there was a bird...

6. And on that bird there was a wing...

7. And on that wing there was a bug...

8. And on that bug there was a germ...

9. And on that germ there was a
   smile...

There Was an Old Lady

1. There was an old la-dy who swal-lowed a fly,

I don't know why she swal-lowed the fly, poor old la-dy, per-

haps she'll die. 2. There was an old la-dy who

swal-lowed a spi-der that wrig-gled and wrig-gled and

tick-led in-side her; She swal-lowed the spi-der to

catch the fly, I don't know why she swal-lowed the fly,

poor old la-dy, per-haps she'll die.

Additional Verses

3. There was an old lady who
   swallowed a bird,
   How absurd, she swallowed a bird;
   She swallowed the bird to catch
   the spider,
   That wriggled and wriggled and
   tickled inside her;
   She swallowed the spider to catch
   the fly...

4. There was an old lady who
   swallowed a cat,
   Imagine that, she swallowed a
   cat...

5. There was an old lady who
   swallowed a dog,
   What a hog to swallow a dog...

6. There was an old lady who
   swallowed a cow,
   I don't know how she swallowed
   a cow...

7. There was an old lady who
   swallowed a horse,

   SHE DIED OF COURSE!
   (*Spoken*)

And Then What?

There Was a Man

There was a man and he was mad so he jumped in-to a pa-per bag.

Additional Verses

2. But the paper bag, it was so thin, that he jumped onto the tip of a pin.

3. The tip of the pin was very sharp, so he jumped onto an Irish harp.

4. But the Irish harp was very pretty, so he jumped onto the back of a kitty.

5. The little kitty began to scratch, so he jumped into a cabbage patch.

6. But the cabbage patch was way too big, so he jumped onto the back of a pig.

7. The little pig began to tickle, so he jumped onto a big dill pickle.

8. But the big dill pickle was oh, so sour, so he jumped onto a big sun flower.

9. Then along came a bee and stung him on the chin, and that was the end of him.

Momma, Buy Me a China Doll

Mom - ma, buy me a chi - na doll,

Mom - ma, buy me a chi - na doll,

Mom-ma, buy me a chi-na doll, Do, Mom-my, do.

Additional Verses

Spoken: Where would we get the money from?

2. We could sell daddy's feather bed,
   We could sell daddy's feather bed,
   We could sell daddy's feather bed,
   Do, Mommy, do.
   Spoken: But what would daddy sleep on?

3. He could sleep in sister's bed....
   Spoken: And where would sister sleep?

4. She could sleep in baby's bed....
   Spoken: And where would baby sleep?

5. She could sleep in the kittens' bed....
   Spoken: And where would the kittens go?

6. They could go to the chicken coop....
   Spoken: And where would the chickens roost?

7. They could roost on grandma's rocking chair....
   Spoken: And where would grandma sit?

8. She could sit in the piggy pen....
   Spoken: And where would the piggies sleep?

9. They could sleep in my own bed....

Let's Go Hunting

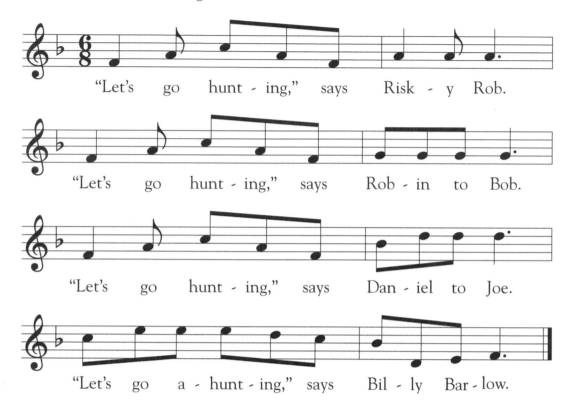

"Let's go hunt-ing," says Risk-y Rob.

"Let's go hunt-ing," says Rob-in to Bob.

"Let's go hunt-ing," says Dan-iel to Joe.

"Let's go a-hunt-ing," says Bil-ly Bar-low.

Additional Verses

2. "What shall we hunt?" says Risky
   Rob.
   "What shall we hunt?" says Robin
   to Bob.
   "What shall we hunt?" says Daniel
   to Joe.
   "What shall we hunt?" says Billy
   Barlow.

3. "I'll hunt rabbits,"....
   "Possum for me,"....
   "I'm chasing racoons,"....
   "I'm chasing rats!"....

4. "How shall we divide him?"....

5. "I'll take the shoulder,"....
   "I'll take the thigh,"....
   "I'll take the back,"....
   "Tailbone mine!"....

6. "How shall we cook him?"....

7. "I'll fry mine,"....
   "I'll boil thigh,"....
   "I'll bake back,"....
   "Tailbone raw!"....

Let's Go to the Woods

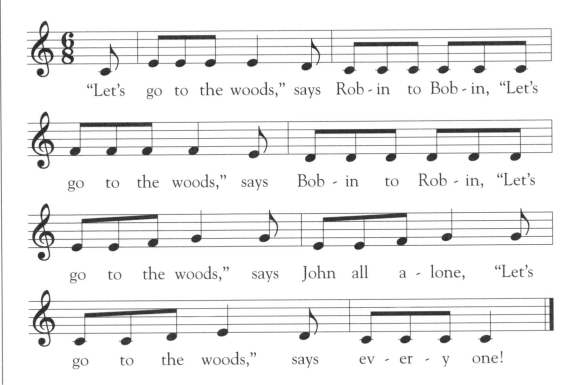

"Let's go to the woods," says Rob-in to Bob-in, "Let's

go to the woods," says Bob-in to Rob-in, "Let's

go to the woods," says John all a-lone, "Let's

go to the woods," says ev-er-y one!

Additional Verses

2. "Oh, what to do there?" says
   Robin to Bobin,
   "Oh, what to do there?" says
   Bobin to Robin,
   "Oh, what to do there?" says
   John all alone,
   "Oh, what to do there?" says
   everyone!

3. "We'll shoot us a wren,"...

4. "How'll we get it home?"...

5. "With a cart and six horses,"...

6. "Who will cook it?"...

7. "I will cook it,"...

8. "Who will eat it?"...

9. "We'll all of us eat it."...

10. "What'll we do with the
    bones?"...

11. "Leave the bones for the
    crows,"...

Three Jovial Huntsmen

There were three jo - vial hunts - men, A -
hunt - ing they would go, And they hunt - ed and they
hal - loed, And they blew their horns al - so.— Look ye
there now, look ye there now.

Additional Verses

2. They hunted and they halloed,
   And nothing could they find,
   But a barn in a field, And this they
      left behind.
   Look ye there now, look ye there
      now.

3. The first he said it was a barn,
   The second he said, "Nay."
   The third said, 'twas a meeting
      house, With the steeple blown
      away.
   Look ye there now, look ye there
      now.

4. They hunted and they halloed,
   And nothing could they find,
   But a stone in a wall, And this they
   left behind.
   Look ye there now, look ye there
   now.

5. The first he said it was a stone,
   The second he said, "Nay."
   The third said, 'twas an egg, That
   the bracket hen did lay.
   Look ye there now, look ye there
   now.

6. They hunted and they halloed,
   And nothing could they find,
   But a frog in a pool, And this they
   left behind.
   Look ye there now, look ye there
   now.

7. The first said it was a frog, The
   second he said, "Nay."
   The third said, 'twas a canary bird,
   With the feathers blown away.
   Look ye there now, look ye there
   now.

Old Obidiah

1. Old   Ob - i - di - ah   jumped   in the   fire   and the

2. - 8.

2. Fire   was   hot   so he   jumped   in the   pot   and the
3. Pot   was   black   so he   jumped   in the   crack   and the
4. Crack   was   high   so he   jumped   in the   sky   and the
5. Sky   was   blue   so he   jumped   in the   canoe   and the
6. Canoe   was   shallow   so he   jumped   in the   tallow   and the
7. Tallow   was   soft   so he   jumped   in the   loft   and the
8. Loft   was   rotten   so he   jumped   in the   cotton   and the
9. Cotton   was   white   so he

9.

slept   all   night.

There's a Hole in the Bucket

There's a hole in the buck-et, dear Li-za, dear Li-za,

There's a hole in the buck-et, dear Li-za, a hole.

Additional Verses

2. Mend the hole in the bucket, dear Georgie, dear Georgie.
   Mend the hole in the bucket, dear Georgie, mend the hole.

3. With what shall I mend it, dear Liza,... with what?

4. With a straw, dear Georgie,... a straw.

5. The straw is too long, dear Liza,... too long.

6. Cut the straw, dear Georgie,... cut it.

7. With what shall I cut it, dear Liza,... with what?

8. With a knife, dear Georgie,... a knife.

9. The knife is too blunt, dear Liza,... too blunt.

10. Whet the knife then, dear Georgie,... whet it.

11. With what shall I whet it, dear Liza,... with what?

12. With a stone, dear Georgie,... a stone.

13. The stone is too dry, dear Liza,... too dry.

14. Wet the stone then, dear Georgie,... wet it.

15. With what shall I wet it, dear Liza,... with what?

16. With the water, dear Georgie,... the water.

17. In what shall I get it, dear Liza,... in what?

18. In the bucket, dear Georgie,... the bucket.

19. But there's a hole in the bucket, dear Liza,... A HOLE!

Oops!

Songs about tricks and tribulations

Bertie Bubble

Bert - ie was a bub - ble who went float - ing in the air, A ve - ry bril - liant bub - ble for his col - ors they were rare, He float - ed past the win - dow, and he near - ly hit the wall, He float - ed through the kitch - en, and he float - ed down the hall.

Verse 2

He was drifting on so nicely, when a
   wind blew through the door,
It shook poor Bertie Bubble, and it
   bounced him on the floor.

Of all the great misfortunes, this
   surely was the worst,
There was trouble for our bubble,
   when poor old Bertie burst.

The Boll Weevil

The boll wee-vil is a lit-tle black bug from Mex - i - co they say, Came all the way to Tex - as, Just a - look-ing for a place to stay, Just a - look-ing for a home, Just a look-ing for a home._____

Additional Verses

2. The first time I saw the boll
   weevil, he was sitting on the
   square,
   The next time I saw the boll
   weevil, he had all his family
   there,
   Just a-looking for a home....

3. The farmer took the boll weevil
   and stuck him in the sand,
   The weevil told the farmer, "I am
   going to stand like a man,
   'Cause I'm looking for a home."....

4. The farmer then took the boll weevil and stuck him on a cake of ice,
   The weevil told the farmer, "This is
   mighty cool and nice,
   And it's going to be my home.".....

5. The merchant got half the cotton,
   and the boll weevil took the rest,
   He only left the farmer just a single
   old ragged vest,
   He had found himself a home....

The Frog and the Crow

A jol - ly fat— frog— lived in the ri - ver swim - o. A come - ly black crow lived on the riv - er brim - o. "Come on shore, come on shore," Said the crow to the frog, and then - o. "No, you'll bite me, No, you'll bite me," Said the frog to the crow a - gain - o.

Verse 2

"O, there is sweet music on yonder
   green hill-o,
And you shall be a dancer, a dancer
   all in yellow.
All in yellow, All in yellow," Said the
   crow to the frog, and then-o.
"All in yellow, All in yellow," Said
   the crow to the frog again-o.

Verse 3

"Farewell, ye little fishes, that in the
   river swim-o.
I'm going to be a dancer, a dancer all
   in yellow."
"O, beware! O, beware!" Said the fish
   to the frog, and then-o.
"I'll take care, I'll take care," Said the
   frog to the fish, again-o.

Verse 4

The frog began a swimming, a swimming to land-o,
And the crow began jumping to give
   him his hand-o.
"Sir, you're welcome, Sir, you're welcome," Said the crow to the frog,
   and then-o.
"Sir, I thank you, Sir, I thank you,"
Said the frog to the crow, again-o.

Verse 5

"But where is the sweet music on
   yonder green hill-o?
And where are all the dancers, the
   dancers all in yellow?
All in yellow, All in yellow?" Said
   the frog to the crow, and then-o.
"Sir, they're here, Sir, they're here."
Said the crow to the frog. (GULP!)

May Day in the Morning

There was a crow sat on a stone, He
flew a - way and there was none. An -
oth - er came and there was one, 'Twas
May Day in the morn - ing.

Verse 2

There was a cat skinned up a tree,
To see whatever was to see.
When he fell down then down fell he,
'Twas May Day in the morning.

Verse 3

There was a rooster in a trough,
Who got a touch of whooping cough.
He sneezed his tail and feathers off,
'Twas May Day in the morning.

Verse 4

There was a farmer made a wish,
That he could swim like any fish.
They popped him in a chafing dish,
'Twas May Day in the morning.

Verse 5

There was a man who grew so fat,
He always stuck in his rocking chair.
It doesn't rhyme but I don't care,
'Twas May Day in the morning.

Michael Finnegan

There was an old man named Mich - ael Fin - ne - gan,

He had whisk - ers on his chin - na - gan, A -

long came the wind and blew them in a - gain,

Poor old Mich - ael Fin - ne - gan. Be - gin a - gain.

Verse 2

There was an old man named
  Michael Finnegan,
He kicked up an awful dinnegan,
Because they said he must not sing
  again,
Poor old Michael Finnegan. Begin
  again.

Verse 3

There was an old man named
  Michael Finnegan,
He went fishing with a pinnegan,
Caught a fish and dropped it in again,
Poor old Michael Finnegan. Begin
  again.

Verse 4

There was an old man named
  Michael Finnegan,
He grew fat and then grew thin
  again,
Then he died and had to begin again.
Poor old Michael Finnegan. Begin
  again.

The Leprechaun

In a shad - y nook, one moon - lit night, A lep - re - chaun I spied, With scar - let cap and coat of green, A can - dle by his side.___ 'Twas tick - tack - tick his ham - mer went, Up - on a tee - ny shoe, And I laughed to think of a purse of gold,___ But the fair - y was laugh - ing, too!

Verse 2

With tiptoe step and beating heart,
Quite softly I drew nigh,
'Twas mischief in his merry face, A
    twinkle in his eye,
He hammered, and in a teeny voice,
He sang a tune or two,
And I laughed to think he was caught
    at last, but the fairy was laughing too!

Verse 3

As quick as thought I seized the elf.
"Your fairy purse!" I cried.
"The purse," he said, 'Tis in her hand -
The lady by your side."
I turned to look; the elf was off! Then
    what was I to do?
O, I laughed to think what a fool I'd
    been, and the fairy was laughing too!

Piggy Wig and Piggy Wee

Pig - gy Wig and Pig - gy Wee, Hun - gry pigs as

pigs could be, For their din - ner had to wait

down be - hind the barn - yard gate.

Verse 2

Piggy Wig and Piggy Wee,
Climbed the barnyard gate to see,
Peeping through the bars so high,
But no dinner could they spy.

Verse 3

Piggy Wig and Piggy Wee,
Got down sad as pigs could be;
But the gate soon opened wide
And they scampered forth outside.

Verse 4

Piggy Wig and Piggy Wee,
What was their delight to see?
Dinner, ready, not far off,
Such a full and tempting trough.

Verse 5

Piggy Wig and Piggy Wee,
Greedy pigs as pigs could be
For their dinner, ran pell mell,
In the trough both piggies fell!

Old Joe Clark

Fare thee well, Old Joe Clark, Fare thee well I say.

Fare thee well, Old Joe Clark, Ain't got long to stay!

I went down to Old Joe's house, Met him at the door.

Shoes and stock-ings in his hands, His feet up-on the floor!

(Chorus)

Verse 2

I went down to Old Joe's house
Never been there before,
He slept on the corn shuck bed,
And I slept on the floor.
(Chorus)

Verse 3

I went down to Old Joe's house,
He told me come and eat,
I drank all the curdled milk
And he ate all the meat.
(Chorus)

Verse 4

Old Joe Clark he built a house,
Told his friends, "It's neat."
He built the floors above his head,
The ceilings under his feet.
(Chorus)

The Tailor and the Mouse

There was a tai-lor had a mouse, Hi did-dle um-kum

fee-dle. They lived to-geth-er in a house, Hi did-dle um-kum

fee - dle. Hi did - dle um - kum, ta - rum, tan - tum,

Through the house of Ram - sey, Hi did - dle um - kum

o - ver the lea, Hi did - dle um - kum fee - dle.

Verse 2

The tailor thought the mouse was ill,
Hi diddle umkum feedle.
Because he took an awful chill,
Hi diddle umkum feedle.
  (*Chorus*)

Verse 3

The tailor thought the mouse would
    die....
And so he baked him in a pie....
  (*Chorus*)

Verse 4

He cut the pie, the mouse ran out....
The mouse was in a terrible pout....
  (*Chorus*)

Verse 5

The tailor gave him catnip tea....
Until a healthy mouse was he....
  (*Chorus*)

Tommy and the Apples

As Tom - my was walk - ing one fine sum - mer day, Some

ros - y cheeked ap - ples he saw on his way.

Saw on his way, Saw on his way, Some

ros - y cheeked ap - ples he saw on his way.

Verse 2

Those apples were ripe and so pleas-
   ant to see,
They seemed to say, "Tommy, come
   climb up the tree,
Climb up the tree, climb up the tree."
They seemed to say, "Tommy, come
   climb up the tree."

Verse 3

So Tommy climbed up; from the
   bough he did fall,
And down came poor Tommy, the
   apples and all,
Apples and all, apples and all,
And down came poor Tommy, the
   apples and all.

Verse 4

His face was all scratched and he felt
   very sore.
He promised he'd never steal apples
   no more,
Apples no more, apples no more,
He promised he'd never steal apples
   no more.

The Tune the Old Cow Tried to Sing

As Farm - er John came home one day, On a

sum - mer's af - ter - noon, He sat right down 'neath a

Chorus

ma - ple tree, To sing him - self a tune. And

this was the tune, right fal - dol - di - do,

Sung 'neath the ma - ple tree. Right fal - lal - fal -

do - ri - day, Was the tune that the old cow died on.

Additional Verses

2. The cows all got around him and
   circled in a ring,
   For they never heard old Farmer
   John attempt before to sing.
   (Chorus)

3. The oldest cow in the farmer's herd
   tried hard to sing that song,
   But she could not reach the melody
   though her voice was loud and strong.
   (Chorus)

4. The farmer laughed till the tears
   ran down his cheeks like cherries red,
   When the cow got mad and tried to
   sing until she dropped down dead.
   (Chorus)

5. Now Farmer John had an inquest
   held to see what killed his cow.
   The jury sat and a verdict brought,
   which I mean to tell you now.
   (Chorus)

6. They said that the cow might be
   living yet, to chew her cud with
   glee,
   If Farmer John hadn't sung that
   song beneath the maple tree.
   (Chorus)

the book of **children's songtales**

Going, Going

Traveling songs

A Ship A-Sailing

I saw a ship— a - sail - ing, a - sail - ing on the sea,— And it was deep - ly lad - en with pret - ty things for me.— There were com - fits in the cab - in and al - monds in the hold;— The sails were made of sat - in and the mast was made of gold.—

Verse 2

The four and twenty sailors that
  stood between the decks,
Were four and twenty white mice
  with rings about their necks.

The captain was a duck with a jacket
  on his back;
And when the fairy ship set sail, the
  captain said, "Quack, quack!"

I'm Gonna Pick My Banjo

Old wom-an in the gar-den, Scratch-in' a-way with the

hoe. I'm set-tin' on the door-step, Mak-ing my fin-gers

Chorus

go. I'm gon-na pick my ban-jo, I'm gon-na pick my

ban-jo, I'm gon-na pick my ban-jo, I'll pick it while I

can. Pick it in the morn-in', Pick it in the eve-nin',

I'm gon-na pick my ban-jo, Right to the prom-ised land.

Verse 2

Old hound, he's just a-restin'
Too lazy to hunt the coon.
I 'spects he's just like I am,
He'd rather hear a tune.
  (*Chorus*)

Verse 3

Old woman, she's so ragged,
She can't run around.
So she has to stay to home,
And bake my hoe cake brown.
  (*Chorus*)

Verse 4

Preacher says I'll never
Reach the promised land.
So I guess I'll stay right here,
With my banjo in my hand.
  (*Chorus*)

I'll Sell My Hat

I'll sell my hat, I'll sell my coat, To buy my wife a lit-tle flat boat. Down the riv-er we will float. Come bib-ble in the boo-shy lo-ree.

Refrain

Shool, shool, shool I rool, Shool I rack-a-shack, shool-a-bar-be-cue. When I saw my Sal-ly ba-ba yeel, Come bib-ble in the boo-shy lo-ree.

Verse 2

I'll sell my pants, I'll sell my vest
To get some money to go out West.
There I think I'll do my best,
Come bibble in the boo-shy lo-ree.
(Refrain)

Over the River *Lydia M. Childs (1802–1880)*

O - ver the riv - er and through the woods, to

grand - fath - er's house we go.— The horse knows the way to

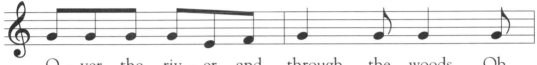

car - ry the sleigh through the white and drift - ed snow.—

O - ver the riv - er and through the woods, Oh,

how the wind does blow!— It stings the toes and

Verse 2

Over the river and through the wood,
To have a first rate play.
Hear the bells ring, "Ting-a-ling-ding!"
Hurrah for Thanksgiving Day!
Over the river and through the wood,
Trot fast my dapple-gray!
Spring over the ground like a hunting
    hound!
For this is Thanksgiving Day.

Verse 3

Over the river and through the wood,
And straight to the barnyard gate.
We seem to go extremely slow
It is so hard to wait!
Over the river and through the wood,
Now grandmother's cap I spy!
Hurrah for the fun! Is the pudding
    done?
Hurrah for the pumpkin-pie!

And That's the End

Cockles and Mussels

In Dub-lin's fair cit-y where girls are so pret-ty, I

first set my eyes on sweet Mol-ly Ma-lone, As she

wheeled her wheel-bar-row through streets broad and nar-row cryin',

"Cock-les and mus-sels a-live, a-live-o."

Verse 2

She was a fish monger, and sure 'twas
  no wonder,
For so was her father and mother
  before,
As they wheeled their wheelbarrows
  through streets broad and narrow,
Cryin', "Cockles and mussels alive,
  alive-o."

Verse 3

She died of a fever and no one could
  save her,
And that was the end of sweet Molly
  Malone.
Now her ghost wheels her 'barrow
  through streets broad and narrow,
Cryin', "Cockles and mussels alive,
  alive-o."

The Carrion Crow

A car - rion crow sat on an oak,

Der - ry, der - ry, der - ry dek - ko;

A car-rion crow sat on an oak, Watch-ing a tail-or

mend his cloak, Sing heigh - o, the car - ri - on crow,

Der - ry, der - ry, der - ry dek - ko!

Verse 2

O wife, bring me my old bent bow,
  Derry, derry, derry dekko;
O wife, bring me my old bent bow,
That I may shoot yon carrion crow;
Sing heigh-o, the carrion crow,
  Derry, derry, derry, dekko.

Verse 3

The tailor shot and missed his mark,
  Derry, derry, derry dekko;
The tailor shot and missed his mark,
And shot his old sow through the
  heart,

Sing heigh-o, the carrion crow,
  Derry, derry, derry dekko.

Verse 4

The sow died and the bells did toll,
  Derry, derry, derry dekko;
The sow died and the bells did toll,
And the little pigs prayed for the old
  sow's soul,
Sing heigh-o, the carrion crow,
  Derry, derry, derry dekko.

The Old Woman and the Pig

There was an old wom-an and she had a lit-tle pig,

mmm - mmm - mmm. There was an old wom-an and she

had a lit-tle pig,— mmm - mmm - mmm.— There

was an old wom-an and she had a lit-tle pig,

did - n't cost much 'cause it was - n't ver - y big,—

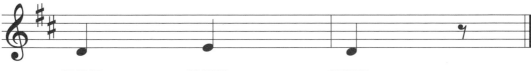

mmm - mmm - mmm.

Additional Verses

2. Now this old woman kept the pig
      in the barn,
      mmm, mmm, mmm.
   Now this old woman kept the pig
      in the barn,
      mmm, mmm, mmm.
   Now this old woman kept the pig
      in the barn,
   Prettiest little thing she had on the
      farm,
      mmm, mmm, mmm.

3. Now this old woman fed the pig on
      clover....
   It laid down and died all over....

4. The little piggy died 'cause it
      couldn't get its breath....
   Wasn't that an awful death....

5. The little old woman, she died of
      grief....
   Wasn't that a sad relief....

6. The little old man he sobbed and
      sighed....
   Then he too laid down and died....

7. Now that was the end of the one,
      two, three....
   The man and the woman and the
      little piggy....

8. The good old book lies on the
      shelf....
   If you want any more you can sing
      it yourself....

Oh, Blue (Version 1)

Had a dog, and his name was Blue, Bet your

life he's a round - er too! Oh, Blue, Blue, Blue, oh, Blue.

Additional Verses

2. Every night just about good dark,
   Blue goes out and begins to bark,
   Oh, Blue, Blue, Blue, oh, Blue.

3. Everything just in a rush,
   Blue tree'd a possum up a white
   oak bush,....

4. Possum walked out on the end of a
   limb,
   Blue set down and talked to him....

5. Blue got sick and very sick,
   Sent for a doctor to come quick....

6. Doctor came and came in a run,
   Says, "Old Blue, your huntin's
   done."....

7. Blue died and died so hard,
   Scratched them holes all 'round in
   the yard....

8. Laid him out in a shady place,
   Rubbed him over with a possum's
   face....

9. Dug his grave with a silver spade,
   Laid him down with a golden
   chain....

10. When I get to heaven I'll tell you
    what I'll do,
    I'll take my horn and blow for
    Blue....

Oh, Blue (Version 2)

I had a dog and his name was Blue,

I had a dog and his name was Blue.   I had a dog and his

name was Blue, and I bet-cha five dol-lars he's a

good dog too.   Here   Blue!   You good dog,   you.

Additional Verses

2. Chased that possum up a hollow
   tree,
   Chased that possum up a hollow
   tree,
   Chased that possum up a hollow
   tree,
   Best huntin' dog you ever did see.
   Here Blue! You good dog, you.

3. Caught that possum up a hollow
   tree, *(x3)*
   Best huntin' dog you ever did see...

4. Baked that possum good and
   brown, *(x3)*
   Laid sweet potaters all around...

5. Old Blue, he died one day, *(x3)*
   So I dug his grave and I buried him
   away...

6. I dug his grave with a silver spade,
   (x3)
   Lowered him down with a golden
   chain...

7. When I get to heaven there's one
   thing I'll do, *(x3)*
   I'll grab me a horn and blow for
   Blue!...

Tooriltetoo

Oh! Too-ril-te-too was a bon-ny cock rob-in, He

tied up his tail with a piece of blue rib-bon, His

tail was no big-ger than the tail of a flea, Tooril-te-

too thought it pret-ty as a tail could be.

Verse 2

Oh! Tooriltetoo was so proud of his
   tail,
To show it off better, he stood on a rail,
An old gray cat came over the wall,
And she ate up poor Tooriltetoo, tail
   and all.

Who Killed Cock Robin?

Who killed Cock Rob - in? Who killed Cock

Rob - in? "I," said the spar - row, "with my

lit - tle bow and ar - row, it was I, Oh, it was I."

Additional Verses

2. Who saw him die?
   Who saw him die?
   "I," said the fly, "with my tiny eye,
   It was I, oh, it was I."

3. Who caught his blood-o? (x2)
   "I," said the fish, "with my little
   silver dish,"...

4. Who sewed his shroud-o? (x2)
   "I," said the eagle, "with my little
   thread and needle,"...

5. Who made the coffin? (x2)
   "I," said the snipe, "with my little
   pocket knife,"...

6. Who dug his grave-o? (x2)
   "I," said the owl, "with my little
   wooden shovel,"...

7. Who lowered him down-o? (x2)
   "I," said the crane, "with my little
   golden chain,"...

8. Who sang the preachment? (x2)
   "I," said the rook, "with my little
   holy book,"...

9. Who carried him to the grave? (x2)
   "I," said the kite, "It was not at
   night,"...

10. Who preached the funeral? (x2)
    "I," said the lark, "with my song
    and harp,"...

11. Who tolled the bell? (x2)
    "I," said the bull, "Because I could
    pull,"...

12. Who was chief mourner? (x2)
    "I," said the dove, "I mourned
    with love,"...

(Make up additional verses.)

Index